T0194195

WHEN YOUR MARRIAGE IS OVER

Practical Advice for
Surviving Divorce and Living Divorced

By Dennis Jacobson

authorHOUSE®

AuthorHouse™
1663 Liberty Drive
Bloomington, IN 47403
www.authorhouse.com
Phone: 1-800-839-8640

First published by AuthorHouse   02/22/2011

ISBN: 978-1-4567-3198-4 (e)
ISBN: 978-1-4567-3199-1 (sc)

Library of Congress Control Number: 2011900643

Printed in the United States of America

*Any people depicted in stock imagery provided by Thinkstock are models,
and such images are being used for illustrative purposes only.
Certain stock imagery © Thinkstock.*

This book is printed on acid-free paper.

Preface

This book is for people going through divorce, for those who know someone going through divorce, for those who have been divorced, and for those people with divorced friends and family members. Divorce happens. It's usually not pleasant. The manner in which a person deals with divorce can make it more or less awful. Less awful is better. This book is about conduct and attitude which can make divorce less awful for you, your kids, and those close to you.

I have been practicing law for 32 years. During the most recent 30 of those years I have represented clients in divorce cases. A substantial portion of my practice has also included defending clients on criminal charges brought against them for conduct arising out of marital conflict that led to the divorce or occurred while divorce was pending. The clients, attorneys, opponents, and situations I have encountered have presented a wealth of observational information that has taught me much about human behavior during and following the divorce process. In this book, I am sharing those lessons with you. I have never been timid about telling other people what they should or should not do, and that is just what this book does. Though I have never been divorced, I have lived through hundreds of divorces. Some were simple and easy. Others took years and were filled with conflict over absolutely every issue. A wise person learns from the mistakes as well as the good example of others.

Introduction.

What most people know about divorce (before they actually experience it) they learned from friends, coworkers, television shows, movies and novels. Most of what they "know" is wrong. Most of what they are told is inaccurate.

There is no national divorce law. Each state has its own substantive law, procedural law, and court system for divorce. Within each state, courts are organized into judicial districts or other geographic groupings, and each may have local rules. On top of that, each district may have multiple judges who hear divorce cases, and no two judges take exactly the same approach. Most issues that judges are asked to resolve in divorce cases are impacted by the discretion, orientation, and personal bias of the judge who hears the case. So to survive divorce, you need to know what happens in your court in front of your judge.

The substantive law of divorce varies from state to state. In some states you need a reason or cause to get divorced. In most states, the only reason you need is that you no longer wish to be married. Some states are community property states and some are not, but all have rules or criteria for property division. Some states have custody and some don't. States whose laws don't use the term "custody" have "parenting plans." Child support is calculated by strict mathematical formulas in some states and is much more discretionary in others. Some states have alimony. Others call this maintenance or spousal support or something else and determine the amount and duration according to a variety of rules, or sometimes just on impulse. To survive divorce, you need to know the language, law and procedure of the jurisdiction in which you live. You can do that through retaining a competent and experienced divorce attorney. It will save you money in the long run, to say nothing of brain damage or jail time. I have had many clients who went cheap on a divorce lawyer or didn't get one at all. They later spent substantial money paying me to clean up the mess - the unclear agreements, the incomplete orders, and the mistakes in what they thought was a comprehensive and clear agreement or order. When it comes to divorce planning, tactics and expectations, talk to a competent divorce attorney experienced in the jurisdiction where your case will be brought. You will be glad you did.

Contents

CHAPTER 1
Kids aren't puppies.

Not everyone going through a divorce has kids. By kids I mean un-emancipated children still at home and dependent on their parents for support. Adult kids are not a part of this discussion. Those who have no dependent children when going through divorce are the lucky ones. But many people going through divorce do have kids, and kid issues are the biggest issues to be resolved. That's why this is Chapter 1. That and because children of any age are very vulnerable to and too often victimized by the bad behavior of their parents during and after divorce. Children know what is going on. They pick up on your conversations on the phone or in the next room. They know what you think of their other parent. Your kids are not your therapist, they are not your parent, and they are not your puppies.

Children don't get divorced, their parents do. The children are not property to be divided nor are they puppies with whom each parent is entitled to " their turn." Unfortunately, many parents involved in divorce suddenly change their whole perspective on their parental role and interaction with their children, insisting on "their turn" or "their fair share" of the time. That is a toxic and tragic attitude that is NOT helpful to the children.

The best attitude to have toward issues of parenting and decision making is to, as trite as it sounds, put the kids' interests first. Most state laws decree that the court will make decisions "in the best interests of the children." But best interests according to whom? The mom whose husband is having an affair with some young woman may think it is in the best interest of the children that they never see their dad. The dad whose wife is aloof, distant, and depressed (probably because of him) may feel it is in the best interest of the kids to be in his care, even if he never gave a bath, changed a diaper, or helped with a homework assignment before the break-up. Both are missing the point. I suggest this rule: Try to preserve the kids' lives as intact and unchanged as possible. Consider the following illustrations that clarify this idea.

Work for continuity.

If dad has always been the soccer coach, he should still be the coach after separation (absent some heinous conduct that renders his involvement inappropriate or impossible). That includes the transportation, the car pooling and other responsibilities and routines that went along with his coaching role. If one parent has been the homework helper, the parenting plan or schedule should reflect that and to the extent possible, seek to preserve that role. No doubt each parent, upon separation, will need to develop additional skills and competencies in areas in which they did not have responsibilities in the past. This learning is going to be a process, not an immediate event. Let the focus be on being a parent, not something else. Do not turn your parenting time into a contest over who the kids will like better. NEVER seek time with the children just to keep them away from the other parent.

Encourage a positive relationship with the other parent.

If you have been and intend to be the primary residential parent for your children, you need to know that it is your job not just to tolerate, but to affirmatively encourage and foster a positive relationship between the kids and the other parent. Deal with it. It is your duty under the law and the right thing for your kids. That means that you don't say to a child reluctant to go to the other parent, " I know you don't want to go, but you have to. I'll be waiting for you when you get back." What you say is ,"I'm sure you and (Mommy/Daddy) will have a great time. You can tell me all about it when you come back on Sunday. Besides, I have to do (some nasty chore the child hates, like cleaning the gutters or scrubbing floors) and you'll be a lot happier with (Mommy/Daddy). Have a great time."

If you think you would gag saying something like that, then you just have to work at it more. Remind yourself you are giving your child a gift- the gift of permission to love, to like, and to have fun with **either** parent. It is a huge gift. It is free, it is priceless, and only you can give it.

Scheduling Activites.

If your child or children have ongoing activities, like a sports team or dance, music, religion classes, swim lessons or the like, the circumstance of which parent's home they happen to be at on a given day should not affect their participation. Too many parents cause their kids to miss a practice, a game, a recital, or a performance because it is scheduled to occur on "their time." That is just wrong. Note: I am speaking here of ongoing activities a child enjoyed prior to their parents' separation. We are after continuity here. Just as each parent should facilitate the continuation of and attendance at these activities, neither parent should start piling on new activities, especially on the other parent's time. As to such activities, TALK TO EACH OTHER FIRST. If both parents agree, then enroll the child and then tell the child. If both do not agree, drop it or ask the court for an order, or if there is a court appointed decision maker (I like the New Mexico term- "wise person") present it to them for resolution BEFORE presenting it to the child.

You need to also think of your children first in planning day to day activities. Even in intact families, possible activities are often brought up and discussed before they become certainties. A simple statement like "Maybe we'll go to the zoo this weekend" can and usually does raise expectations that this weekend you really will go to the zoo. Then something happens, or nothing, and the outing doesn't take place. Children are disappointed. It's even worse when this happens with children of divorce because added to disappointment is contention and fault finding. Here is how this problem plays out: Dad calls daughter who is at mom's to tell her that he has tickets to the stage production of *The Lion King* for Saturday, but it's not his parenting time. He'd like to take daughter, but only if its ok with Mom, because it is on Mom's time. Daughter then asks Mom if she can go. Daughter really, really, really wants to go, but Mom's grandfather is turning 100 and there is a big party planned and great grandpa doesn't have much longer, so Daughter is told no because she will be with Mom and they have plans. Now Daughter is angry at Mom, Mom is angry at Dad, Daughter will probably act out at great grandpa's party and then everyone will be mad at her, and Dad. And it's all Dad's fault in this example. Why? Because he discussed a possible event with Daughter before clearing it with Mom. The whole mess was completely avoidable.

Whether you think great grandpa's 100ᵗʰ birthday should trump *The Lion King* is not the issue. The issue is that Dad should have talked to Mom before even mentioning the activity to Daughter. Read that again. Then learn and follow this rule: NEVER MENTION AN ACTIVITY TO YOUR CHILD THAT WILL TAKE PLACE ON THE OTHER PARENT'S TIME UNTIL YOU HAVE FIRST TALKED TO THE OTHER PARENT AND RECEIVED THAT PARENT'S CONSENT FOR THE CHILD TO PARTICIPATE. That goes for both parents, mom and dad, regardless of who has the most time with the children. If you love your kids and want them to salvage the best possible life from the wreckage of what was your marriage, follow this rule.

Creating a Workable, Child Friendly Parenting Schedule

Some of the worst problems pertaining to parenting time following or during divorce come from poorly written and vague parenting schedules. Follow this rule: *Every event has a starting date and time and ending date and time.* If you think that is too anal and that reasonable people can get along and play fair, then you are asking for trouble. Reasonable people will follow the rules (see Chapter 8). What if the parenting schedule says Dad has the kids on Father's Day and Mom has them on Mother's Day? That seems clear enough, but what time do these events start and end? Does the visiting parent get 24 hours or an hour? Is it an overnight? Does it tack on to weekends? Another issue arises because Mother's Day and Father's Day are always on a Sunday. If the parents are alternating weekends, and the special day falls on the other parent's weekend, what governs? Is it the holiday rule or the regular weekend schedule? Spell it out in your agreement or Order.

The simple issue of parenting time on Mother's Day and Father's Day can be further complicated by rules for special summer parenting time. If each parent can designate uninterrupted summer parenting time, can Mom select time that includes Father's Day? Your parenting plan, whether by agreement or Court Order, must spell out what rule takes priority when there is a potential conflict. If the judge didn't do this in the Court Order, ask the judge to do it. If the court still refuses, ask another judge. It's that important.

My preference is that summer vacation time trumps regularly scheduled parenting time, and the holiday schedule trumps everything. There is no second choice. By the way, I think Mother's Day and Father's Day are appropriate overnight events, if each parent is getting overnights, and I would write that holiday parenting time agreement like this:

Father will have parenting time with the children for Father's Day each year from 6 pm the Saturday immediately preceding Father's Day through 7 pm on Father's Day, a total duration of 25 hours.

The last little phrase makes it clear that the event is not a week long, it's a day long. Us a little additional ink, and a few more words and the agreement removes any possible ambiguities. You will be glad you did. Follow the same rule for defining a weekend. It starts on a certain day and time and ends on a certain day and time. Be just as precise for every parenting event. <u>Every event.</u>

Creating a child friendly schedule means not going crazy over holidays, except for Christmas, if the parties observe it. Kids can have a bunch of different Christmas celebrations and love all of them. I suggest each parent be allocated at least 72 hours on or near the holiday each year, if the children are of appropriate age. The parties can alternate the allocated times each year so one party doesn't always get Christmas Day or Christmas Eve. I also favor exchanges that take place after noon if on Christmas Day, and if I had my way there would never be an exchange on Christmas Eve after about noon on that day. Let your kids stay up late, sleep in, and avoid the stress of having to hurry to get somewhere. If the parents live more than a short car ride apart, then read Chapter 10 which deals with that circumstance as a holiday schedule consideration. In my experience, kids can never have too many Christmases- mom, dad, 2 or 3 or even 4 sets of grandparents, cousins- the more the merrier. But kids should only have to have one Thanksgiving. In my experience, splitting up this holiday weekend is evil. The event for kids usually starts when school is out on Wednesday and continues to Sunday night. It's a long enough time for a quick trip out of town to ski, go to the beach, or visit family. Even if you are not going anywhere, Thanksgiving weekend, as all right thinking people know, is for giving thanks, overeating, lying around, sleeping in, playing or watching football, and maybe, for the energetic, going for a walk. It is not for rushing around. I suggest this event be alternated so each party has it every other year, Wednesday after school (say 6:00 p.m.) until Sunday at 6:00 p.m.

Regarding holidays, your birthday is **not** a holiday and neither are the kids' birthdays. New Year's Eve and New Year's Day are not really viable as separate holidays and don't mean very much to kids as separate events. Let these days merge with the Christmas plans. In contrast, Spring Break (and Fall Break, if the kids have one separate from Thanksgiving) are holidays to deal with in the parenting schedule, and if the family and kids have made it important, so is Easter. Avoid special rules for all the Monday holidays- let them tack on to the parent's weekend by adding 24 hours to the regular weekend schedule. Even if it seems one parent is getting all the good three-day weekends, the fact is that the allocation of these holidays will even out over 7 year stretches. If there is a special event, you can always agree to deviate from the schedule, and should. Of course, if your family celebrates traditional Jewish holidays and festivals, or those of Islam or another faith, deal with them in this same way- focus on the substantial events and let the minor ones just fall where they fall.

Flexibility

Every parenting schedule should open with the words "Unless otherwise agreed by the parties, the following schedule shall govern." In every divorce there will be occasions when deviation from the set schedule should, or even needs to occur. So what should you do when your former spouse asks for a piece of your holiday or weekend parenting time? The answer is, be reasonable. Keep records and create a writing to document every deviation from the schedule if it is very substantial. Also, it is always appropriate to expect and to ask for equivalent make up time as a condition of the deviation. The usual thing to do is to trade time. Suppose Mom's family is having a reunion over Labor Day Weekend, but it's Dad's parenting time. If Dad has no plans, and it really is a big deal, he should agree to let the kids be with Mom, BUT Mom should return the consideration by adding to Dad's time in the immediate future or agreeing to give him one of her upcoming three day weekends or otherwise provide make up time, **if Dad wants.** Dad doesn't have to require make up time, but he is entitled to do so. Agreements to deviate from the parenting schedule are made all the time. Unfortunately, the parent getting the extra time does have a tendency to forget the deal when it comes to payback. So write down the arrangements made and the make up time that will be given. No one should be insulted by being asked to do that. You might even consider including a provision in the parenting orders that deviations from the schedule have to be in writing. Being reasonable doesn't mean agreeing all the time, or even ever, if circumstances justify declining a request to deviate. If you are the parent asking for the time, and it is declined, you are not entitled to a reason, or an argument, or to be bitchy. Let it go. Follow the orders. Of course, you will remember the turn down when you are asked for an accommodation. Keep a log of requests granted and requests denied going each way. It will show things are not as awful as you think, and it may be useful if continual frustration causes the issue of deviation to end up in a court action. Be guided by the overriding principle of maintaining the most normal life and schedule for your kids.

Don't badmouth the other parent

Kids aren't puppies. If they don't have the appropriate professional credentials, they also aren't therapists.. Many people going through divorce don't understand this. They "vent" to their kids, they want to "share" frustrations, and they want to "talk through" problems that really don't involve the kids. It will be almost impossible to avoid some of this, but you can minimize it. If you are a person who needs to talk through problems concerning yourself and your ex-spouse or your future ex-spouse, do it with someone other than the kids. That person can be a professional therapist (good idea) or a special adult friend (if they are willing and tolerant and very patient).

You do not need to tell the kids everything that is wrong with your spouse and you should not. You do not need to justify yourself to your children. You can't. Your children, if over the age of about 2 ½ years, have a pretty good idea of everything they need to know or want to know about your marriage and your life. Spare them. Sometimes children will bring up issues such as why you separated, who is that man or woman I saw you with at the soccer game, or even raise complaints about the other parent. I think parents need to be good listeners but also guide kids away from such conversations (unless there is a report of abuse or severe neglect being made, in which case notes should be taken and authorities notified.)

One useful approach when a child brings up issues like those listed in the preceding paragraph is to use the "you've given me a lot to think about" line and then say you'll think about what they have said and you can talk later. Then move them into some fun and distracting activity. Often the subject is never raised again. If it is, deal with it in the most positive and limited way possible. Sometimes, believe it or not, one parent will send the kids on a mission to ask questions of or engage the other in conversation to spy on them or save the cost of a private investigator. So be alert to that. Relieve the kids from their mission by moving them off the subject. Your children will be relieved. Of course, age appropriateness is important here. Conversations with 17- year- olds may not have to be limited in the same fashion as those with a 9- year- old. However, it is never a bad thing to move off the negative and over to the positive with children of any age.

Kids aren't puppies. They are people, feeling their own distress in the divorce. In all things, try to let them keep their lives as intact as possible and they will love you for it.

Chapter 2
God is on my Side.

Maybe it is the times in which we live, but even reflecting back 30 years, I recall very few divorce cases in which religion was a major issue. However, when it becomes an issue, it can be a huge complicating factor and source of conflict, both for the parties and for the children.

The first premise in dealing with religion as an issue is to follow the premise set forth in Chapter One about striving to maintain continuity in the lives of the children. If for years the kids have been active in a church or church school, and its activities, they should continue. That seems easy enough, and fair, but when one spouse has chosen to leave the marriage contrary to the tenets of the faith the family subscribed to and the church they all attended, that parent can feel rejected, threatened, even vilified. I recall a case where the mom left the dad for reasons most people would find justifiable. They had a ten year old daughter who when visiting with dad on alternate weekends continued going to his church, which was not a mainstream group. Every time the daughter was at dad's church (which had been mom's church too) she was told by the church members that her mother was possessed by evil or the devil. Even more devastating was their habit of expressing condolences as they told her that when the child went to heaven, her mother wouldn't be there. Mother would be in hell forever. Oh, and have a nice day.

I think faith is an important aspect of life, and I am slow to criticize anyone who incorporates their faith and religious practice and participation into their life as an significant component. I do that. However, I do have a problem with groups that would find it appropriate to inflict pain on a child in the manner that those words must have done. If you are active in a religious or faith community that feels compelled to terrorize children in this way which can turn on its members so suddenly, you might want to rethink the child's participation there. You might stay active, but in a different local body where there is no history with your ex-spouse. At the very least, you must shield your child from such venomous attacks. Even if the speakers hold such statements to be true, there is no point in inflicting them on a child who loves her mother.

If the question comes up, there is only one response that I think is appropriate. If someone in your church or faith community (or family or social network)feels compelled to point out the eternal condemnation of your former spouse, I suggest you tell your child that you love them, their other parent loves them, and God (or Allah or Jehovah or Jesus, or Isis or the Great Spirit) loves them too and God (et al) will sort it out. Read them an appropriate excerpt from your faith's sacred texts. There are plenty to support your statements. Then move off the subject and engage your child in a different direction.

Many people who subscribe to a given faith or who are members of a particular church or faith community aren't really up on the finer points of that faith, and may know little or nothing about the actual doctrines and beliefs of their religion pertaining to divorce.

I recall a 40-something –year- old man who met with me years ago. He was a member of a fundamentalist Christian church, and he wanted to get divorced. The second time we met, he brought in his new girlfriend, a member of the same church, and she was also married. They each wanted me to represent them in their respective divorces. What was remarkable to me was the part of the conversation in which the woman told me how she just knew God was drawing them together, and that she could feel God's hand in what was going on. I happened to be active in that same denomination (grew up in it, in fact) and was pretty familiar with Biblical texts on divorce, infidelity and the like, and if God's hand was in it according to those texts, God's hand was there to offer a dope slap.

The tragedy of the "God told us to divorce our spouses and marry each other" couple is that each had kids who had been raised in that church, had friends in that church, and had come to adopt the beliefs and doctrines of that church. Now their parents were acting in a way contrary to the entire belief system the children had been presented by those parents. These parents were also claiming divine blessing for acting in a way that was at odds with what they had been presenting to their children for years. The point here is that you and your family are better served to leave God out of the conversation about divorce. If your beliefs are based upon a sacred text, you might want to be familiar with those texts. If your beliefs are Biblically based, be reminded that Biblical texts say God hates divorce, but tolerates it in some cases. They also say God's forgiveness is unlimited, so there is a balance. On this point, a comment from Abraham Lincoln is instructive. He was commenting on the Civil War (and what is divorce if not a civil war?) and stated that both sides, North and South, proclaimed that God was on their side and their cause was just. He then observed that one side must be, and BOTH sides may be, wrong. So too in divorce.

Some people who are served with divorce papers do not believe divorce is ever appropriate, or certainly not in their case. They resolve through prayer and preaching to the court to keep this divorce from happening. Rather than engage the issues, they deliver their protestations and then pretty much just let the divorce happen to them. That is a big mistake. Divorces are heard in the civil courts following human rules created by legislatures and applied by judges, not priests or pastors or imams or rabbis. Divorces are not heard in ecclesiastical courts. They are held in secular courts where sermons and prayer are rarely allowed and invariably ignored. If you feel you are the "victim" of divorce, you need to minimize that victimhood by engaging the issues, retaining competent counsel and working toward a fair result. If you don't, you will be disadvantaged and hurt economically. Your kids, if you have them, will be hurt, and you will likely turn into a bitter, lonely person who ends up questioning the faith that you proclaimed as a reason not to fight. Whether you are a Catholic, Muslim, Baptist, Mormon, Jewish, Pagan, or any other faith, you can respond in a divorce action without forfeiting your soul or your integrity. That is especially true if you follow the suggestions and directives contained in this book. It's fine if you select an attorney who shares your religious views, but select a lawyer first based upon experience and competence. That is more important than whether or not they share your faith.

One last area that needs to be addressed in this chapter is the "prayer list." The fact is that in any social group, including a church or faith community, your divorce can be a source of entertainment and diversion for others. People will talk about it and about you, and once you put yourself or your family on the prayer list, you are suddenly in the public domain. People will give you "the look." People will suddenly stop talking when you enter the room. I told you already that my faith and my church are important to me. My pastor can be a helpful counselor and sympathetic friend. However, I keep my pastoral needs between me and him, and he is discreet. I recommend the same for you. No one has to abandon their faith or beliefs during or after a divorce. They don't have to use them as weapons either.

Chapter 3
Who's on your team?

Chapter 2 ended with a warning about not airing your divorce business or personal life too broadly. I stand by those comments. However, you will need a team, a limited number of people in whom you can confide. Your lawyer is on that team, but lawyer's rates are higher than a therapist's rates, so if you just need to vent, or cry, or get support coping, a professional licensed therapist is appropriate. That therapist will be on the "need to know" or "ok to vent to" list. Staff persons at your lawyer's office are on the team, but don't be surprised if you are billed for your conference time with them. It is customary and usual to bill for paralegal time, and some lawyers bill other staff time. However, paralegal rates are usually 25% to 40% of attorney rates so if you need to vent and don't have a therapist, vent to the paralegal.

There may be other professionals- business appraisers, vocational evaluators, tax experts, etc. - involved in your divorce but they aren't on your inner circle team. Let your attorney and staff deal with them. Those people are generating information and argument, and are not your personal confidants. Their job is not enhanced by having you tell them everything wrong with your spouse or ex-spouse.

In cases where orders concerning children are in dispute there may be a custody evaluator. These people are known by other titles as well, including child and family investigator, parenting time evaluator, special advocate, wise person, or something else. Their role is to interview the parties, the children, personal references, observe the parties and children together and apart, and make recommendations to the court. They are not in your inner circle of confidants either. Chapter 4 deals with interacting with these people.

In addition to the professionals on your team, I think everyone should have one person to dish everything to or on. It can be a bff, a relative, or a co-worker, but there should be just one person, known for their discretion and ability to keep private matters private. Such a person is a wonderful asset and a rare commodity. If you have a person like that, be sure to repay their patience, kindness and support in a meaningful way, as often as you can.

That's it. Your lawyer, the lawyer's assistant, a paid therapist and one close friend. You get to talk divorce with them, but don't do it with others. There are several reasons. First, people will gossip. When they do, they will not retell your circumstances accurately, and sooner or later misinformation will circulate back to your home and to your kids, and that is bad. The next reason to limit your circle of intense "sharing" on divorce issues is that your friends will get tired of it and of you. You will wear them out. You will be accused of being the king or queen of depression, and people will avoid you. Those that run away from you will talk about you, and not in a good way.

Another reason to limit your divorce sharing is that if you talk to too many people, you are without question going to hear about the person they know who went through divorce and what that person did. You will hear all kinds of information and suggestions which will include a substantial portion of misinformation and bad advice. It might be bad legal advice, but it is just as likely to be bad personal advice. There are a lot of people going through divorce who, over the course of their case, spend hundreds if not thousands of dollars on attorney time telling their attorney what "this guy they know" had to say on one issue or another. Rarely, if ever, has any lawyer received useful information or insight from these anonymous sources.

The next reason to limit those with whom you share the details of your divorce is huge. If you get in the habit of talking about divorce issues or your ex's issues with just about everyone, you will have a hard time turning off that fountain when the kids are around. , Your kids don't need and don't want to hear that kind of conversation, not from you and not third hand from a gossipy friend. Your kids, even adult kids, should not be part of the inner circle of "sharing all."

A final reason for not sharing too much with too many people is that the more you say and the more people you say it to, the more likely it is that something you said will come back to hurt you in some way. Imagine being in a custody trial and hearing testimony about something awful that you said about your spouse, or a child, or the evaluator. It happens and it can be devastating.

Your navigation through a divorce and restoration to normalcy afterward will be made much easier by keeping the details and drama of the process exposed to a limited number of people, most of whom have a professional obligation to maintain your confidences. Make every effort to limit your communication as much as possible to those on your team. If people press you to share more, just tell them your lawyer told you not talk about it, and then steer the conversation in some other direction.

Chapter 4
The Custody Evaluator

In most states, either party or the Court can seek a professional evaluator to do an investigation and study and make recommendations to the Court concerning the issues of parenting schedules and decision making responsibility for the children. They may also focus on other child-related issues such as education, relocation and the like. As noted in Chapter 3, these people can be known by many names. Regardless of their title, the simple truth is that their opinion carries substantial weight with the Court. It is also true that different evaluators take different approaches to their work, and some have known biases or leanings. Many people will offer opinions about different evaluators, usually baseless and misguided, so discuss the selection with your lawyer. Your lawyer should know most of the evaluators in your area as well as their biases and prices. If your lawyer doesn't know about the evaluators in your area, that is a pretty good indication you should have a different lawyer. Costs for these evaluations vary. In my practice they presently average about $9000.00, with low cost ones going about $5000.00 and high conflict cases or those with unique issues running $20,000.00 or more.

Evaluators will be watching you and listening to you even when you think they are not. They are observing to see if all those things your spouse and his/her parents said about you are true. They are looking for signs of anger and bitterness, parenting skills, ability to encourage the children in their relationship with the other parent. They will look into driving history and criminal records, mental health issues, and other stuff I still haven't figured out in 30 years. I have arrived at a few useful tips in dealing with an evaluator. Here they are.

1. **Be punctual**. This is always appropriate. Nothing else needs to be said. Besides, you may be charged for the time the evaluator waits for you. That missed time will also come off your allotted time and you will have less time to present yourself and information you want to share with and have considered by the evaluator. Lack of punctuality also says something about your organizational skills in general and parenting skills in particular.

2. **Do your paperwork and submit it in a timely fashion.** In nearly all cases there will be forms to fill out for the custody evaluator. These will include areas like family history, marital history, personal references, and what you think the parenting plan should be. How you respond to these written inquiries, the timeliness of submission neatness and responsiveness, are all reflections on you. They will have a significant impact on the evaluator's recommendations. Fill out all written inquiries thoughtfully, with insight, focusing on the children. Don't be impulsive, vitriolic, and obsessed with making sure the evaluator knows every negative thing about your spouse. Everything you write is on the record, so take your time, be thorough and be positive.

3. **Use personal references that have seen you interacting with your children.** As obvious as this may seem, some people don't get it. They give as references their supervisor or coworkers, teacher or yoga instructor, teammates on their bowling team, or someone else who has rarely if ever seen them with the children. It is much better to present the kids' coaches, your neighbors, play group parents, or anyone who sees you and your children together on a regular basis. Tell your references you have listed them and why they are involved, and then stay out of the way. Avoid "coaching" references or trying to write their comments for them. It is unnecessary and not very useful. It can also be counterproductive. Don't do it.

4. **Pay your share of the fee in a timely manner.** We all want to believe something as unrelated to kids and parenting as non-payment will not affect an evaluator's recommendations, but it can and it does. Something about punctuality of payment, just as in the case of punctuality for scheduled interviews, seems to enhance credibility and likeability.

These are both traits it is good to have the evaluator ascribe to you. Even if the evaluation was asked for by your spouse, courts usually apportion the initial payment of fees. Pay your share in a timely fashion. If you want to argue the fairness of the allocation, do it in court at a later time.

5. **Speak in terms of the children, not yourself or your spouse.** This is a subtle but important aspect of conveying information to the evaluator and later to the court. Instead of saying "I read to little Johnnie every night" try and convey the same information by saying "Johnnie loves to be read to. He particularly likes the Beatrix Potter books, so we read one together every night at bedtime." If you are talking about sports, instead of saying " I've coached little Joanie's soccer team for the past four years" try saying " Joanie loves playing soccer and is close to all her teammates. As her coach, I have seen how she has really grown athletically and socially through her soccer." In each case, the same information is given, but the child is the focus, not you. This same approach can be used when, if you feel you must, conveying a negative about the other parent. Instead of saying " Johnnie's dad never reads to him," you might say " Johnnie takes books to his dad's house, but we usually read them at home because reading at bed time is just not something his dad is in the habit of doing. " Or you could simply say " I am sure little Johnnie would like his dad to read to him too. I hope dad develops a bed time reading habit. He didn't do much of it when we were together." You get the idea. It's about the children so let them be the subject of your sentences.

1. **Use "sad."** When talking with an estranged spouse or ex-spouse, a judge, or when talking or writing to a custody evaluator, avoid words like "hate", "mad", "upset", "irritated" and the like. I think the word "sad" is a great substitute. It conveys thoughtful depth of feeling and child focus. Consider these two communications:

    Option 1 "I hate it when little Billy's dad is late picking
    him up. I work hard to get Billy to go on a visit
    and when his dad is late, it destroys all my hard
    work."

    Option 2: "It's very sad when Billy's dad is late for
    parenting time. Billy looks forward to seeing his
    dad, and we prepare for the visits together as I

encourage Billy in his relationship with his dad. When he is late, I can see the disappointment in Billy's eyes. If a schedule change would help dad to be able to be punctual I'd be glad to consider it for Billy's sake."

I hope you find that the second option is more appropriate. I think you get the point, but to give an example from another context, consider these two sentences:

Option 1: "I get really frustrated and angry when Joanie's mom doesn't send proper clothes with her on a visit."

Option 2: "It's very sad when Joanie comes for a visit and doesn't have appropriate or sufficient clothes. Can you suggest what I can do to help eliminate this problem for Joanie?"

I have been through hundreds of divorces over three decades and have had plenty of time to work on this kind of communication approach, but you can do it too. Just remember, you are never mad, angry or upset. You are sad. "Angry" and "mad" are not words that describe a really nurturing parent. But to have something that pains your child cause you sadness, well, you must be a sensitive parent, tuned in to your child's feelings and needs.

2. **Know about your kids and demonstrate that knowledge.**
   You should know and be able to call to mind without notes the following information about each child:

Name, date of birth, place of birth

Favorite food, favorite color, favorite book, and favorite movie (as age appropriate) and favorite TV show

Best friend's name, address and best friend's parents' names

Other friends' names and addresses and their parents' names

Teachers' names- regardless of how many teachers the kids have

Primary doctor's name, dentist's name, other regular health care providers names,

addresses and telephone numbers

Last time each child went to the doctor and to the dentist and why

Each child's favorite subject in school (as age appropriate)

Each child's favorite sport or activity

Coach or teacher for child's sports and activities

What social networking sites each child has and the passwords for each

Names and addresses of the parents of your child's boyfriend or girlfriend (if they have one)

Educational and professional goals and aspiration of each child (as age appropriate)

Parents who do actual parenting know these things. You need to know them too. If you don't know them already, learn them and demonstrate that knowledge to the evaluator.

8. Be truthful. My father used to say to me that the best thing about telling the truth is that you don't have to remember what you said. The next best thing is you don't get caught in a lie and lose all credibility and thus inflict a serious wound on your chances for obtaining the kind of parenting plan you want. Lies can consist of withholding of information as well as giving false information or even just making things up. Sometimes there may be a question in a party's mind about disclosing remote events about which no one involved in the case is aware, such a juvenile or criminal offense occurring years before you were married or a period of mental health counseling in the distant past. If in doubt, discuss the matter with your attorney. But if your spouse, kids, family members, in-laws, parole officer, probation officer or neighbors are aware of something, you better disclose it before they do. What you see as the most negative points need to be addressed up front and openly so the evaluator can resolve them and move on.

9. Write your own report after each session with the evaluator. Send a copy to your attorney and keep a copy. The evaluator is writing things down, and so should you. Your court hearing may be months away, and an accurate record of important events and comments that you create as they happen and are fresh in your mind is priceless. Once the evaluation is done and a report is issued, it is not only possible, it is likely that at least some of the reporting will have errors and you will need to correct them. Reference to your notes will help you do that.

10. Be a reporter, not an editor. There is a big difference between giving information and arguing. To clarify this point let us assume you are the mother of a nine year old boy who returned from a weekend visit with his father and reported to you that dad has magazines with pictures of naked women in them. Let us assume this upsets you and you believe it to be inappropriate, so you call the evaluator and say, " Jim has magazines at his house with pictures of naked women in them and little Johnnie saw them. That's not right. Little Johnnie should not be exposed to that environment." What you said was not a report because what you conveyed was not attributed to Johnnie and your statement contains information you assumed but that Johnnie did not report. Because you do not know the basis for Johnnie's comment, you could be and probably are way off the mark. What really happened in this little example is that Johnnie and his dad stopped at a neighbor's house to pick up mail because dad had been out of town, and the neighbor was holding a magazine with the offending cover. As they left the neighbor's house, Johnnie had asked his dad if he ever had a magazine like that, and Dad answered yes. This really happened. It's a true story. Mom didn't lie in the sense of conveying knowingly false information, but she was pictured as an alienating parent who blew things out of proportion. The evidence against her came from her own lips. She assumed the worst, made an erroneous report to make Dad look bad, and in fact was engaged in parental alienation. Report what you know and your source of knowledge. Don't try to fill in the corners or draw conclusions.

11. Don't bad mouth the other parent. That's someone else's job. That's what you are paying your lawyer to do, in part. In dealing with the custody evaluator, feel free to provide relevant information about the other parent that may be negative, such as their criminal record, alcohol related traffic offences, smoking and drinking habits, but only report objective and verifiable facts. The one thing you do not want to be is a purveyor of parental alienation. Evaluators will have their antennae up to detect any hint of trying to turn the kids against the other parent. The dad who refers to the mother of his children as a bitch or whore or stupid or lazy or unstable or a drunk or a pot head or by some other similarly terse character-assassinating terms better have objective evidence to prove his characterizations or he is only hurting himself. The hardest thing to avoid is calling the other party a liar when confronted with their lies. Speak to the issue, not the person. Rather than saying "she is a liar," say "that statement is not true." Some people going through divorce are obsessed with verbally attacking, belittling and denigrating the other parent. They do not come out well in parenting disputes. Stay child focused and fact focused.

12. Don't think the evaluator is your therapist. While they may have professional degrees and licenses in psychology or social work, the evaluator is not *your* therapist. There is no confidentiality pertaining to your communications with them. Their purpose is not to help you feel better or to mediate disputes. Their role is to collect information about the parties and children in order to formulate recommendations to the Court to enter orders that will govern your relationship with your children for years to come. Answer their questions, fill out their forms, and conduct yourself appropriately during all meetings with them, following the suggestions in paragraphs 10 and 11.

Chapter 5
Where Did They Hide the Money ?

Before the marital assets can be divided in a divorce proceeding, all property needs to be identified, located, valued, and listed as marital or separate. The identification of property as marital or separate can be cause for serious argument, but generally speaking, separate property is property a party owned before the marriage or received during the marriage as a separate gift to one party or an inheritance left to one party. If a party has separate property but then places it in joint title or puts separate cash in a joint account, that property will usually lose its separate character and be treated as marital property. The process of locating and identifying property often leads to the conclusion that some is missing. Usually what is missing is cash, like the $30,000.00 a party took from savings days before filing for the divorce. Rules and laws governing divorce require each party to make a thorough disclosure of all assets, but some people still try to hide money on the "don't ask don't tell" theory of disclosure. That is, if asked about something they will disclose it, but if not asked they won't. If you think your future ex- is hiding money, talk to your lawyer, and as part of the inquiry have them look into each of the following fairly subtle places to stash assets.

1. **Lawyer's trust account**. A person going through divorce may try to secret funds by giving their attorney a large retainer. Funds on account with legal counsel should be disclosed as an asset but aren't always listed as such. Make a specific request for information on any retainers paid to counsel or other experts. You are entitled to it.

2. **Overpayment of taxes or over-withholding of taxes**. Self employed people are supposed to file quarterly tax estimates. Sometimes a party will seek to hide or stash some extra money by overpaying those estimated taxes, especially if part of the divorce arrangement or orders designate that the parties file separate taxes for the year in which their divorce was final. If a self-employed accountant or lawyer or therapist or masseuse is a quarterly estimated tax payer and actually expects to owe $10,000.00 for a quarter but pays $25,000.00 in estimated taxes for that quarter, the government will not inquire, but you should. Ask for all estimated tax payment information and line it up against receipts and expenses and prior years' tax payments and liability. Your lawyer will get all that information. Focus on the overpayment.

For salaried workers with multiple dependents and other itemized deductions, changing the withholding from married with four dependents to single with zero dependents will result in a pretty substantial accumulation of marital funds as overpaid taxes in the name of that party. Be sure to look for any changes in W-4 designation (the withholding form filed with the employer). If there is no change in filing status but there seems to be over-withholding in prior years which is continuing, call that to the attention of your attorney. You are entitled to your fair share of overpaid taxes no differently than your fair share of a joint savings account, regardless of from which party's salary or wages the taxes were withheld.

3. **Phantom purchases**. In most cases you will be looking at up to 3 years of cancelled checks, credit card statements and debit card statements on all accounts of each party. Most of us pay the same people or businesses on a regular basis and new or different purchases stand out rather clearly. Sudden payments to a mechanic never used before may be fictitious, with cash kicking back to the party who claims to have made the payment. The same may be true for other purchases or even purported debt repayment to parents or other family members or friends. Look for the new and unusual expenditures as you seek to uncover efforts to hide assets.

4. **Check their pockets**. There was a particular divorce action in which I took the deposition of the other party. Both parties and their lawyers were seated around the conference table. A court reporter was taking down all of my questions and the respondent's answers. About an hour into the examination I asked the respondent what he had in his pockets and briefcase (he had a briefcase with him and was dressed in a

business suit). The Respondent protested, but, at the urging of his attorney, answered. I thought his answer was deceptive, so I asked him to empty everything from his pockets and open the briefcase. In addition to over $1500.00 in cash, there was a cashier's check payable to the respondent for over $30,000.00 and a valuable assortment of precious stones and gold coins. All together, over $50,000.00 in assets were on the Respondent's person. I got lucky that day. Now, when I take a party's deposition, I always ask the deponent to disclose the contents of their pockets and briefcase. You never know what you might find.

5. **Question the business books.** Many people getting divorced have businesses that take in a lot of cash and it's easy to avoid reporting all of it. If you suspect that there is some "under the table" payment going on, you may need a business expert or auditor to look for changes in patterns of cash accounting or deposits. If you have personal knowledge of past practices, share them with your attorney.

6. **Be thorough in your requests**. Even if the other party lies and fails to disclose information, you still want to be exhaustive as to your information requests. The reason for this is that if any asset information that you requested is not provided, or any assets known to the other party are not otherwise disclosed, when they are later discovered the innocent party will have an action against the non-disclosing party to recoup a reasonable portion of the undisclosed asset. The circumstances of each case will dictate what level of inquiry is appropriate. Two wage earners with limited assets who have been married for a year will not need the same extensive investigation and inquiry into assets that parties to a divorce involving a business or a professional practice, a long term marriage, multiple investment accounts, and high cash flow will require.

Chapter 6
Full Disclosure Full Disclosure Full Disclosure

The laws of most states require that a party in a divorce action provide the other party complete and accurate information about all assets, debts, and income sources. In this digital age it is very easy to obtain information of this kind. Even if you think you can hide assets (see Chapter 5) a court will enter any orders it feels are necessary to see that both sides receive all of the information that they are entitled to receive. My advice is don't try to hide assets. You probably won't succeed. There are remedies available to your ex-spouse even if the assets aren't discovered until years after the divorce and the damage you will do to yourself when your deception is discovered will outweigh any advantage you think you may have gained in hiding something.

I am aware of many creative accounting practices and business organization "stacking" techniques that are used to minimize tax exposure. Stacking, as I use that term here, is when a person forms multiple business entities, each owning some or all of other entities, all in a holding company or limited partnership, or some other multi-level structure. The party owns something but it is disguised or hidden or perhaps just hard to see through all the business structures. It's best to cut through the smoke and mirrors and just disclose what you own in accurate and simple terms.

There are many outstanding lawyers who disagree with me on this point, who will disclose what they have to, and use the law to shield all they can. This is sometimes effective, I suppose. However, in those cases the parties end up fighting in court over information requests, incomplete responses, and other disputes just to learn what property there is to be divided. Each party can spend tens of thousands of dollars just on those issues, to say nothing of the time and emotion expended in the process. Consider all costs as you determine what you may be trying to shield. Rarely, if ever, is it worth the effort to try and hide assets.

I am not suggesting that a party to divorce should not seek to obtain the best possible financial result they can within the bounds of the law. I am saying that in order to do so you should be businesslike and thorough. Demonstrate to the court that you are candid, have made full disclosure, understand the rules and are playing by them. This is really important if you are the spouse who makes the most money or has the greater knowledge of the marriage's finances and assets. It becomes even more critical when you are the overwhelmingly stronger economic party and have controlled the family finances. In fact, not only before a judge but before the other party and their lawyer (as well as your own) you will improve credibility, facilitate meaningful settlement discussion, and avoid unnecessary animosity by disclosing everything . There is plenty of conflict in any divorce without compounding it by playing games with financial disclosures.

As you are assembling and preparing financial information for your attorney and the other side, be aware that income according to tax returns is NOT the same as income for purposes of determining child support or maintenance or other issues in divorce. Don't think for a minute that it is. That is why when you are providing copies of tax returns to the other side, you need to submit the entire return, including all schedules and forms sent to the IRS and state tax departments. Insist on receiving these documents from the other party and provide them yourself, with both personal and business tax returns. Your taxable income is a lot less than your total income. Some deductions from income that the tax laws allow for business owners may be added back to determine your income in the divorce court. These may include things like accelerated depreciation, automobile allowance , food and entertainment expenses, deduction for a home office, and others.

If you have a question about what to disclose or not disclose, ask your competent, insured attorney and follow the lawyer's advice. Then any consequence of a bad decision is the lawyer's. The lawyer will (or should) know what must be disclosed and can evaluate the impact that any particular information may have on outcomes. They will also know the timelines for providing the information to the other side. It is important to not only make full disclosure but to do so in a timely fashion. If you are contemplating divorce, one of the things you should do in preparation is to assemble all personal and business financial records for the past three years plus any documents substantiating any claim you have for separate property. Make a copy for yourself and a copy for the other party. Doing this will save you substantial time, legal fees and aggravation during the divorce. When anything changes, such as a pay raise, paying down a bill, or incurring new debt, update your information. It's not only required, it is a good idea, and it is in your best interest.

Chapter 7
Other Money Games People Play

Apart from trying to hide or failing to disclose assets, there are other money games parties to a divorce play that are ultimately useless and time consuming This kind of conduct will invariably result in unnecessary legal fees and costs, aggravate judges, and have a negative effect on the perpetrator. In extreme cases a stay in jail for contempt of court could be the result. This chapter is a **DO NOT** chapter. Here are several things parties to a divorce **SHOULD NOT DO.**

1.   **Do not neglect paying child support.** If you have the money, pay your child support before all other debts. If times are tough and you can't pay all of your support, pay as much as you can. Never pay nothing. Child support is a debt that cannot be discharged in bankruptcy. If you don't pay it when due, the unpaid amount draws interest at a pretty high rate (1% per month compounded monthly, or even more). In addition, garnishments to collect past due support can take as much as 55% of the net take home pay from those who owe past support. Tax refunds can be intercepted by support enforcement agencies and applied to the delinquent support, and in some jurisdictions you can even lose your driver's license if you owe past due child support. There are also many other nasty things that happen to those who don't pay court-ordered child support. If a contempt of court action is brought, a judge will find the payer could in contempt if the payer had the ability to pay the support but chose not to do so. That means the non-payment was willful. The person owning the support will have to pay up, *and* they will have to pay the other party's

legal fees and costs of collection, in addition to their own lawyer's fees and costs. In extreme cases, a court can sentence the willful non-payer to a jail sentence of up to one year.

2. Do not neglect paying alimony. If you are under a court order to pay alimony (also called maintenance or spousal support in some jurisdictions) it should be given priority over all other debt payments except child support. Alimony, like child support, cannot be discharged in bankruptcy. Also, assuming some very basic criteria are met, maintenance payments are tax deductible by the payer and taxable to the recipient. To be tax deductible, the order must provide for periodic payments (as opposed to a single lump sum), the obligation to pay must terminate on death of either party, and it must also terminate in the event of the remarriage of the recipient. All of the comments on child support in the preceding paragraph apply to alimony payments as well. If you can't pay it all, pay all you can and catch up as soon as possible.

I am often asked, "If maintenance ends if the recipient remarries, then what happens if the recipient just moves in with an intimate partner, shares a house and a bed and acts just like they are married?" In most instances, maintenance is still owed. However, a case might be made for a reduction or abatement if the law of your state factors the contribution from the roommate as "income." Talk to your attorney if this situation arises, but don't hold your breath. Until the court order is changed, your obligation to pay continues

3. Do not surprise the other party with short or late child support or alimony payments. If for any reason you are not able to make a full child support or alimony payment when due, tell the other party as soon as you are aware of the problem.

They (and perhaps your kids) are relying on those funds, and it is the fair thing to do to let the recipient know if there will be delay or shortfall. Surprisingly, a little notice can and does go a long way toward keeping these matters out of court. In a high conflict divorce, with an angry and vengeful ex-spouse, being a day late or a dollar short can lead to the recipient filing an enforcement action with the court. At the very least, they will have their lawyer write your lawyer a nasty letter that your lawyer will read, call you to discuss, then respond to, all the while charging you for the time at their hourly rate. So make a call or send an email if you are going to be a little short or a little late (but don't make a habit of either). That simple gesture may save you hundreds if not thousands of dollars.

4. Do not withhold payment to get your way. If you owe child support or maintenance, those obligations are separate and not contingent upon you receiving your scheduled parenting time or any additional time. Yet there are those people who use money as coercion to obtain a change in schedule, additional parenting time or some other concession. That is just wrong and can lead to grief. Unless you enjoy spending thousand of dollars every few months going back to court over compliance issues, don't do this. It is NEVER appropriate to withhold court-ordered payments, even if your ex is messing with your parenting time. If that is happening, call your lawyer and file an action to enforce the parenting schedule. But know this. One of the first things a court will want to know when a party asks the court to make the other party comply with court orders is whether or not the moving party is in compliance with the orders. If they are not, they may be denied any meaningful remedy. If you have withheld child support or maintenance payments, you are not in compliance with those orders. This is called the clean hands doctrine. Simply stated, it say that if you want to obtain sanctions against the other party for not complying with court orders, you sure better be in compliance with all orders yourself. End of discussion.

5. Do not fight the wage assignment. If a party who receives child support or maintenance wants it paid by payroll withholding, pretty much every state provides that mechanism for payment. It is not punishment to have your child support or alimony paid by an income assignment. Federal law says your employer may not take any action against you because of it. Income assignments relieve the payer from the responsibility of payment so long as they remain in their present employment. It is a good thing for all concerned. Yet there are still those who file Motions and spend lots of money opposing such income assignments, and rarely will they be successful. Let it go.

6. Do not let incorrect income assignments endure. Child support and maintenance payments are likely to change one or more times over the duration that such payments are to be made. When that happens, the recipient and/or their attorney needs to immediately file an amended wage assignment. This is true whether the amount to be withheld goes up or goes down. Often there is a delay in the filing or effective date of the amended wage assignment and an overpayment or underpayment may occur. If there is an overpayment and you received it, refund it to the payer quickly. If there is an underpayment and you are the payer, make up the difference as due. You are obliged to do so. There will come a time in every case when child support ends, and in most cases there will come a time when maintenance ends. When it does, cancel the income assignment, and refund any overpayments as received. You are not entitled to retain the overpayments. Refund them without even being asked. Make the world a better place.

7. **Do not pay late just to aggravate your ex.** Payments received on or before the due date are on time. The payer has no obligation to pay early, even if they have had a habit of doing so in the past. A payment a day late is late and is a violation of the court orders. As noted earlier in this chapter, a violation of court orders can result in punishment, sometimes quite harsh, but still there are people who will express their anger with their ex-, or a toward a child, not by withholding payments due, but just by being a little late. DON'T DO IT. If you don't like the person your spouse or ex- is dating, or are mad at a child for not wanting to visit with you, tell somebody, but don't make late payments to express your anger.

8. **Do not keep your raises and bonuses a secret.** Circumstances change. Incomes fluctuate. People get laid off, fired, or are furloughed and the reduction in income can and usually will, under these circumstances, justify a decrease in child support or alimony. At the very least, a suspension of some or all of the current payments may occur until times are better and the payer can catch up. Similarly, if a payer receives a raise or a bonus, wins a major lottery prize or has other increased income, child support and alimony will likely be increased. Changes in the recipient's income can also impact child support and alimony, though usually in a less significant way. If your income changes more than just a token amount due to an ongoing salary or wage increase, a job change or termination, or a bonus or other windfall, you should report that fact to the other party. You are entitled to the same report from them. Have this duty formalized in the settlement agreement or court order. When people voluntarily exchange information, they avoid the expense of paying a lawyer to request it formally, or going to court to get an order to compel the disclosure.

9. **Do not refuse (or forget) to sign titles, deeds and tax forms.**

If you are ordered to sign something, sign it without delay and without trying to extract some concession for doing so. These kinds of games can lead to time consuming and expensive court enforcement actions, always at the expense of the party who did not do what they were ordered to do. Whether it's a car title, property deed, refinancing papers, a tax form for claiming a child as a dependent or any other document, if you have been ordered to sign it, sign it. Do this without prompting. Or you can get your lawyer involved (for a fee). It's a good idea once the divorce is final to list all of the "to do" items and take the initiative to follow up on each item. As discussed in Chapter 12, the job isn't over until the paper work is done.

Chapter 8
Follow the Orders

People going through divorce or who have been divorced have orders that govern what each party is to do. There are orders for child support, orders for parenting time, perhaps orders to pay certain bills, maintain life insurance, maintain health insurance, pay uninsured health care costs, pay alimony, and so on. There may also be orders to provide to the other party financial information and changes in financial or other circumstances, such changes in day care costs or providers, changes in health insurance cost or coverage, and changes in income. These are **orders,** not suggestions, and they are the law of your case. If you do not comply with the orders, bad things can happen, from having to go back to court and get dressed down by a judge to having to pay your own lawyer *and* the other side's lawyer fees and costs. In extreme cases, you could even be sent to jail.

Everyone should read their divorce orders regularly and put on their calendar when any actions are to be accomplished. Do this whether the action required is to make a debt payment, provide information to the other side, go to a meeting, pay child support or maintenance or do something else. Then you need to follow up and actually do what the orders say *without being prompted*. Your lawyer will happily send you a reminder of upcoming performance requirements, for a fee. Save some money and do it on your own. If you do not perform as ordered, it is close to certain that the other side's lawyer will send your lawyer a notice of non-compliance. Your lawyer will read it (for a fee) and call you or forward it to you (for a fee) and then discuss it with you (for a fee). They will respond to opposing counsel (for a fee). All those fees add up to hundreds or thousands of dollars, money you can use for many other and better things. You will save a lot of money, a lot of time and a lot of hassle by reading your orders and doing what they say in a timely manner. You are going to have to comply with them anyway so avoid causing yourself the additional headache of being made to do so.

Sometimes divorce orders will impose future obligations on a party that are infrequent or sporadic. These obligations may include reporting changes in day care costs, reporting changes in income, providing a copy of a tax return each year, showing proof that life insurance is in place, or providing copies of uninsured health care costs or other expenses for the children in order to receive reimbursement. With regard to some of these obligations, the opposing party may not push ongoing compliance, but you are better off if you calendar the task and always comply within the time period required. Just because the other party doesn't demand compliance immediately does not relieve you of your court-ordered responsibilities. Sooner or later some event will likely occur that triggers a demand for performance from the other party, and your past omissions, though without objection from the other party up to that point, will likely become a cause to vilify you, or even be grounds for a contempt action against you.

On this subject of following court orders, I want to comment specifically on orders for submitting uninsured health care and other expenses for the children to the other party. Many divorce orders provide that the parents share uninsured health care costs per a given ratio, either equally or in proportion to income. Such expenses can be modest in some months, substantial in other months. If you want the other party to pay you promptly, you should submit these expenses together with receipts or proof of payment **every month.** The best written orders and agreements specify that you do so. Those orders should require that the party who incurs the expense must submit it to the other within 30 days of the expense being incurred, **and** that the other party must then pay their share of those expenses within 30 days of receipt. If the expense is really substantial, that is over some specified amount stated in the agreement or order, then it is appropriate to provide that payment *or payment arrangements* be made within 30 days of receipt of information from the other party.

People who save up expenses for several months, or even a year, should expect delay in receiving reimbursement for submitted expenses, and not complain about it. People who submit the expenses each month are much more likely to be reimbursed by the other party promptly and without a big fight. I know of one case in which the parties, by agreement, exchange health care and other expense documentation one time each year for their two active school-age boys. Each submits thousands of dollars in expenses apart from already substantial health care costs. Each year, before payment is accomplished, there are months of discussion and objections, letters and emails between the attorneys, resulting in substantial time, money, and emotion spent on resolving issues that likely would not arise if the expenses were submitted monthly. So if your order says submit monthly, do it. If the order is silent, submit monthly. If the order says to submit expenses less often, think about having it changed.

Some orders are subject to modification by the court at the request of either party and some are not. Those that are modifiable include any orders concerning children (support, parenting time, health insurance, tax deduction, etc.) and some maintenance orders. All of these kinds of orders can also be modified by agreement of the parties. Other orders, such as those concerning property and debt division, are not normally modifiable after a specified period of time absent agreement of the parties. Unless or until an order is modified by the court, it remains the law of your case. Read it, learn it, live it. You don't have to love it, just do it. Do it as a favor to yourself.

If you and your ex do agree to deviate from the orders, that is totally appropriate. If the deviation is minor, such as trading weekend parenting time one time or accepting a payment late, no formal action is required. However, if you agree to modify an ongoing obligation or order affecting recurring events, then you must write down the agreed upon modification and submit it to the court for the court to enter as its order. If a court order says to sell a house and divide the proceeds equally, but the parties later agree one of them will keep the house in exchange for a payment to the other party, that agreement needs to be written and submitted to a court.

The same thing is true of any modification of child support or maintenance payments. If it was not written down and filed with the court, it never happened. The orders will be enforced as written. Each child support and maintenance payment that is not paid when due is a final judgment and cannot be retroactively changed. It is as if the payer was sued on the debt and a court order entered saying they lost the case, they owe the money, and the recipient can use all legal means to collect it. That includes wage garnishments, attaching bank accounts, seizing other property, and similar actions. There is at least one government agency in each state that monitors and collects these payments for the recipient, and they act based upon the existing court orders.

If two parties agree to reduce child support from $400.00 per month to $200.00 per month but never formalize that agreement in the court records, here is what can happen. A few months after the agreement, the primary parent applies for and receives public assistance. That continues for 24 months. Then the government decides to initiate action to recover the benefits paid by enforcing the child support order. The payer has been dutifully paying the $200.00 per month as agreed for the past 30 months. However, the court orders say he should have been paying $400.00 per month, so he is 30 x $200.00, or $6000.00 behind. Adding interest on the accumulating arrearages at 1% per month compounding monthly, the payer now owes over $6500.00. That money will be collected from him or her. However, if the parties had filed a modification of the order with the court at the time they agreed to the change this would not happen.

The same situation occurs when parties just agree to change support or maintenance terms even if no public assistance is ever received. Consider these facts: Dad is paying $1100.00 per month to Mom for the support of their two kids. Mom remarries a very wealthy guy and tells dad that she doesn't need the support money. She tells Dad he should just put the money in a college fund for the kids. Later, let's say 30 months later, dad does something to really upset mom, so she initiates an action to recover 30 months worth of unpaid child support at $1100.00 per month plus interest. That comes to about $38,000.00 and Mom will likely collect it. Even if Dad can convince a court that there was an agreement and he followed it (which is uncertain at best) he will still spend thousands of dollars in defending the claim against him. The same thing will happen if Mom told Dad to forget the child support and did not impose a condition of putting the money in an account for the kids. The lesson is clear. Follow orders just as they are written. If you have an agreement to change the orders do so in a writing filed with the court and made an Order of the Court. Then follow that order.

If you are unsure if an agreement to deviate from the orders needs to be written and filed with the court, ask your lawyer, if you still have representation. If you are not represented at the time the issue comes up, then follow this rule: ALWAYS write up the agreement and file it with the court asking it to be made the Order of the Court.

Chapter 9
The new "Friend"

Some people file for divorce because they have a new love interest. Some people file for divorce because their spouse has a new love interest. Sometimes one or both spouses acquire a new love interest while the divorce is pending. Sometimes one or both acquire a new lover after the divorce is final. If the parties have no children, the new lover is more of an annoyance than a complicating factor. In those cases, how a party reacts to and deals with their spouse's new lover is totally within their control. Too many people overreact. They might have "letting go" issues, even though you might expect that a new love interest would reduce attraction to the estranged or ex-spouse. In my experience, ignoring the new lover is the only appropriate reaction. However, some scrutiny on spending related to that person is appropriate, as discussed later in this chapter. Here we are speaking of cases where there are no children involved. As to those cases, here are some reasons to just let go and not get into a tussle over the new lover.

The first reason to just let go is that by doing so you will avoid being arrested and going to jail. Many people will introduce or flaunt a new lover in front of their estranged spouse just to upset the spouse or get a rise out of them. This often works and sadly can lead to threats, throwing things, throwing punches, public profanity and loud arguing, or worse. Police everywhere give priority to arresting people who perpetrate a crime against a spouse, former spouse, or intimate partner. These offenses are called "domestic violence," and many states require an arrest, jail stay and court appearance for those accused of such an offense. Jail is not a fun place and an arrest is not a good thing to add to your resume.

If you are charged with a criminal offense, once the charges are brought, it is up to the prosecutor to move forward. The alleged victim in many jurisdictions does not get to choose whether or not to "press charges" and cannot "drop charges" even if they wish to. This is true whether the victim is the spouse or the spouse's new lover. The same general rule holds if the " victim " is a car that has had some creative prose scratched into the paint or other property is damaged or defaced.

The second reason not to react to the fact that the other party has a new lover is that if you do, you are giving the other side just what they want. If your spouse wants to get a rise out of you, and they succeed, they win that little battle. Your response distracts you from dealing with the substantive issues in a sane way. The court will most likely learn of the event (your spouse will be sure to share the news) and it won't help your credibility with the judge. Beating the crap out of the new lover might make you a hero with your drinking buddies or book club friends, but that is about the extent of the positive outcomes. Months and months of domestic violence classes, hundreds, if not thousands, of dollars in fines and costs, more legal fees, plus paying for damages and a possible stint in jail all add up to a bad deal.

Another reason to just ignore the new lover is that you need to not care. You have a new life to begin, new financial challenges to overcome, and new people to meet. Invest your time, treasure and talents in yourself, those you love, and those who love you, not the one person on earth about whom you should care nothing. The more time and energy and emotion you spend on your future ex- or ex-spouse the less you will have to spend on yourself and your new life. I have had many clients who acted out over the new lover publically and ended up being arrested. I have had clients who spent hours telling me how unfair it was that their spouse was enjoying the company of the new lover while they languished as a single parent. If you need help getting over your ex-spouse, get some assistance from a well qualified and competent counselor. Hit a pillow with a foam bat if you have to. It's not as satisfying as hitting your spouse with a real bat, but the consequences are more manageable. I am sure there are many other reasons to avoid being provoked to active anger or rage by your spouse's new lover, but I will leave the issue with this brief discussion.

Now let's look at the flip side. Suppose YOU are the one with the new lover. My suggestion is that you not flaunt that person or that relationship when your spouse or ex-spouse is around. There is no value to doing so. If you are so insecure that you feel compelled to demonstrate to your (ex-) spouse that there is another person on the planet who accepts you after you were rejected by them, then you should consult a mental health professional. While your spouse may go to jail if they act out in a confrontation over your new lover, you could end up in the hospital. Moreover, many domestic violence cases end up with BOTH parties getting arrested and jailed and taken before a judge. By creating a high stress and provocative situation, you put yourself and your new companion at risk along with your spouse or former spouse. So do yourself a favor. Don't create stressful situations or problems that don't have to exist. Enjoy the relationship for what it is - a new relationship that fills a void.

And what about the new lover? If that is you, keep away from the divorce proceedings. Don't go to court. Don't go to mediation. Don't go to settlement conferences. We are talking about cases where there are no kids involved, lucky for you. Keep out of it. You and your new companion will be glad you did.

In most divorces that do not involve kids, the presence of a new lover is irrelevant, BUT the manner of spending, sometimes called "wasting" the marital estate, is relevant to division of assets. If you have a new lover on whom you are spending a lot of money before the divorce is final, expect that to be a factor in the division of property. If you spend thousands of dollars on a vacation for you and your new friend, or buy that new friend expensive gifts, that information is discoverable and you should expect a court to treat those expenditures as an advance to you of a portion of your share of the marital property. That means if you spent $10,000.00 on your new lover, your spouse may well get $10,000 of martial assets off the top before the rest of the marital property is fairly divided between the parties in whatever manner the court determines is fair. That is something you need to know. Once the divorce is final, how you spend your money is your own business. While the divorce remains pending, how you spend your money is everyone's business.

All of the considerations shared so far in this chapter also apply to cases in which the parties have minor children, but additional issues arise when there are kids involved. The big question is when and how to introduce your kids to that new lover. I invariably recommend to my clients who are going through divorce or who have been recently divorced that they not introduce their new lover to the children unless and until there is an actual engagement, and a wedding date has been set. Not all of my clients like that advice but once it is explained , most of them come to agree with me and most abide by the suggestion. Now that you are curious, I'll tell you why this is a good rule to follow.

Obviously, if you are dating a drug dealer or child abuser or registered sex offender, if you don't keep him or her away from the kids, you will never be the residential parent. Most people get that. If a party to a divorce is dating someone who fulfills their needs (love is blind, after all) but that person does not fit the conventional view of acceptability or appropriateness for being around children, that party needs to do a good job of isolating that part of their life from the kids. The more difficult situation to deal with is that one where you are dating Mr. or Ms. Wonderful. You don't want to keep that person from your kids but you need to do it. If your kids meet this new person, they will love your new companion and bond with them. If , within a few weeks or months you break up with that person, you subject your children to the loss of someone who has become close to them, perhaps just as they are coming to cope with the divorce of their parents. Your kids may even hate you for that. And if the pattern keeps repeating they will never trust you. For that reason, even the really great, flawless, generous, kind and loving new lover should be isolated from the kids until you know that it is a relationship that is anticipated to endure. For me, that means marriage. Marriage is a pledge of commitment and an expression of intent to be together always. It may not always work out, but the mutual expression of that intent is important and meaningful.

While I stand by my recommendation to not involve the kids with your new love interest until a wedding date is set, the right time for you to introduce you kids to your new love interest may be impacted by how long you have been divorced from their other parent, the kids' ages, and the nature of their interaction with the other parent. However, it is NEVER appropriate to bring your new lover into the children's lives while the divorce is pending.

The situation where a dad brings his new girlfriend with him as he picks up the children for parenting time and has her join the group trip to the zoo while the divorce is still pending baffles me. In my experience this is much more a "husband thing" than a "wife thing," and someone could probably earn a doctorate studying and writing about this phenomenon. All I can offer are my observations as a lawyer as to why this occurs. The first and most frequent reason I observe for dads bringing their girlfriends on parenting time events with the kids while a divorce is pending is that the dad wants validation. They want their kids to see that a nice adult female can like their dad, and dad is not as horrible as mom might be saying he is. Dad has some issues, and in this case he is using the kids as therapy to feel better about himself. Sometimes the validation sought is validation of the relationship with the new lover. Dad's thinking may go something like this : "If the kids like her, then its ok for me to be sleeping with her even though I'm still married to their mom." There are so many things wrong with that thinking that I can hardly contain myself when I hear it from a client. Please, don't do this to your kids. If your date is a wonderful person the kids will love her. Then later when you break up they will hate you. The date's presence will upset mom (who will most certainly be told about her by the kids) and mom will hate you, maybe take it out on the kids a little by being testy or short with them and probably create hassles around your parenting time. Don't do that to your kids. Don't to that to yourself.

It's called parenting time for a reason- it's time for you as the parent to be with your kids: to play, to talk, to do homework, to engage in sports and other activities. When you bring along someone else, your attention, time and some of your money is diverted from the children. This holds true for moms as well as dads. Use your parenting time to be a parent. Develop your personal life, your love life, when the kids aren't around.

Perhaps the closest thing to a valid reason for a party to bring their new lover along on parenting time is that the parent cannot handle the kids by themselves. A mom who is anxious about the young kids overnighting with dad might actually feel better about it if the new

girlfriend is a mom too, and has caretaking skills dad doesn't. Most likely, though, mom will be very upset at the intruder injecting herself into the kids' lives. In addition, dad is essentially confessing his incompetence. A father who cannot take care of his kids without help needs to develop the necessary skills or else limit his parenting time requests to those consistent with his or her limited competence.

If there are children involved in your divorce, the court will need to know about all aspects of the children's lives when they are with each parent. That includes other adults who will be spending significant time with the children, and that means the new girlfriend or boyfriend. This person may be interviewed by a custody evaluator, asked to submit to psychological testing and maybe drug testing. The appropriateness of injecting this new person into your relationship with the children is also a factor to be evaluated. The presence of this new person in the dynamics of parenting exchanges will raise the stress level substantially. Can I be any clearer? Your new lover has no place in the lives of your children while the divorce is pending.

Some readers may be are thinking of a situation where your kids already know the new lover and already have a relationship with that person. Maybe that person has even been a caregiver for the kids. If that person is the children's nanny and you are having an intimate relationship with her/him, then you better get a different nanny, to say nothing of preparing for a potential sexual harassment lawsuit. If that person is the brother or sister of your spouse, or some other relative or close family friend, all I can say is attempt, if possible, to keep the quality, frequency, and nature of the kid's interaction with that person as close as possible to what it was before your intimacy occurred. That may or may not be possible. If you are sleeping with your wife's sister or husband's brother, my guess is that the dynamic of the kids' relationship with their aunt or uncle is probably going to change. If those relationships can't be close to pre-separation normal, then have the new lover drop out of the kids' lives for the present. Your kids don't need the added stress of having your new relationship waved in front of them, especially if their other parent thinks your new lover is evil incarnate.

Your kids do not need to know about or be confronted with your new lovers. They do not have to endorse or condemn your behavior unless you force them to do so, and if you do that, you deserve the judgment you will receive. Your kids aren't getting divorced. They want to love both parents and should be encouraged to do so. Shoving your lover in their faces or your spouse's face undermines that possibility. If you love your kids, spare them the stress. Your new lover will understand. If they don't, then you will have to choose- the new lover or your kids. It's that simple, at least while the divorce is pending.

Chapter 10
Moving Away

We live in a mobile society. It is not unusual for a family to move two or three times, or even more from the time their first child is born until the youngest leaves the nest. People who are divorced move too. Sometimes the moves are compelled by a job transfer, medical necessity, or financial pressures. Other times the move is a choice made to improve quality of life, change lifestyle, be closer to aged family members, or for higher quality schools. Sometimes these moves are within a single town or region, but some result in divorced people living hundreds or even thousands of miles apart.

When a divorced person moves and no minor children are impacted, the move may still affect the other party if one party is making maintenance or periodic financial payments to the other. Enforcement and collectability of those payments, in the event enforcement action becomes necessary, may be a bit more complicated than it would be had the move not occurred. It may be necessary to engage counsel in the state where the paying spouse has moved. In some cases, court orders, from the court where the divorce orders originally entered may then need may then need to be filed in a separate action in the state to which the other party has moved. Enforcement of the orders will then be carried out in the courts of the state to which the paying party has moved. However, the problems are usually minimal, and can be overcome with the assistance of competent counsel.

In cases where there are minor children, most states do not allow the children's primary residence to be moved out of the state where they resided at the time of the divorce unless there is a written agreement of the other party or an Order of the Court. Even in-state moves that are of a sufficient distance to impact the performance of a parenting schedule may, in some cases, require written permission of the other parent or an Order of the Court. A parent who plans to move but not take the children with them can move without the other party's consent and does not need a court order. However, in those cases, the parties should cooperate to create a new parenting schedule which can be a carried out given that moving parent's new residential location.

Consider this example: A divorced couple has two children, ages 10 and 13. Both children are in a public school district that follows a traditional calendar. The kids start school in late August and get out in early June with a ten week summer break. They have a week-long spring break in late March each year, a four-day Thanksgiving recess, two weeks off from late December to early January. The children also have a variety of other days off, most of which are Mondays and Fridays. Before one of the parents moved, the kids were in mom's primary care and dad had parenting time every other weekend from Friday after school until Monday morning, and every Tuesday from after school (or 4 pm in summer) until 9 pm that same day. In addition, dad is provided four days in later December or early January, every other spring break, every other Thanksgiving break, and some Monday holidays allowing him to have some three-day weekends with the children. Each party also 1s allowed a two week uninterrupted period with the children for vacation travel or any other use they chose during the kids' summer break. Then a parent moves away. They move about a thousand miles away, and the schedule no longer works. It needs to change.

On these facts, it is fairly easy to create a new schedule that affords dad about the same time that he had before, but that time will have to be taken as longer events on a less frequent basis. Presuming each party resides in a place with a nearby airport, what makes the most sense for a new parenting schedule is to add time to dad's summer parenting time, expand his year-end time a little, give him spring break each year, and allow parenting time when he is in the area where the kids reside with their mom (with prior notice and assuming there is no conflict with some pre-existing plan). Reasonable people should be able to work out a new plan on these facts, and skilled mediators who have assisted on this type of issue

46

in the past can be helpful if the parties are unable to reach an agreement just working by themselves.

If a parent has more substantial parenting time than in the prior example, then the moving parent who does not have primary care of the children is going to have to accept the fact that with school-age children, that parent is going to get less parenting time after they move than they had before the move. Consider the case where the moving parent has had parenting time with the children every other week or some equivalent schedule where they are with him (or her) nearly half of the time. One parent is moving but is not asking to move the kids' primary residence with them. The logistics of distance and school schedules will impact parenting time. In most jurisdictions, kids go to school about 36 weeks per year. That leaves 16 weeks, more or less, in which to focus travel and parenting time unless you are close enough to pick up some three-day weekends as part of a new schedule. Even if the parent who moved away gets all of the summer and all of the breaks of one week or more in length during the school year, they are still going to realize a substantial reduction in time.

A court is not going to give 100% of the non-school time to one parent. Nor is the primary residential parent likely to agree to that kind of schedule. If you are the parent moving away, I suggest you focus settlement discussions or court arguments on achieving a schedule that does not disrupt the children's school year, allows the other parent a chance for a two week vacation or uninterrupted time with the kids when school is not in session and is composed blocks of time of a week or more. Week-long spring break or fall break events present an opportunity for quality parenting time. The visiting parent should also focus on obtaining at least a week, maybe longer, during the school holiday break in December and January, and an expansive summer schedule. Other events can be included depending on distance between residences and cost and mode of travel.

When developing a parenting schedule that entails travel between the parents' remote households, be aware of possible weather impact on travel in certain locations at certain times of the year, and plan accordingly. Flights can be delayed in the northern and central part of the country due to severe and sometimes prolonged winter storms. From late June through November, the Southeast and Gulf Coast areas can be impacted by hurricanes. These weather phenomena are not the fault of your ex-spouse, so don't react to weather related delays or inconveniences as if they were. DO plan ahead, especially if children are flying unaccompanied. Always have a contingency plan for delayed or diverted flights.

When the non-primary parent moves, issues of enforcement of child support orders from one state to another can also emerge, but there are government agencies, interstate compacts, and other mechanisms that facilitate enforcement of support orders of one state against an obligor in another state. The move should not create any real problems.

The most difficult moving situation with which divorced parents have to deal is when the parent with the primary care of the children wants to move with the children to a new location. As noted above, such a move requires the written agreement of both parties or a court order. If there is agreement, there is no issue. If there is not agreement, then a court will determine if the moving party can move with the children and what the new parenting schedule will be. A new schedule will be needed if the primary care parent and children are allowed to move. It will also be needed if the court disallows the move of the children but the moving party chooses to move anyway without relocating the children. This does happen, but rarely.

Cases in which a parent seeks to move out of state with the children are often emotionally charged, as the non-moving party sees the attempted move as a direct attack on their relationship with the children and worries (with justification) that the move will have a negative effect on that relationship. These removal cases can also be quite costly in time and money as well. Often the conflict becomes a battle to be won for purposes unrelated to the best interests of the children. In some cases opposition to a move is well grounded and may be seen by the court to have merit. In other cases, the chances of the move being allowed are so substantial that the non-moving parent is better served investing their time, treasure and energy in the creation of a workable parenting schedule rather than opposing the move. While no one can predict the outcome of any one particular case on facts that are not known, a few valid generalizations about these cases can be noted.

You must present a valid, substantial and compelling reason for the move that is not just a personal preference. If you are the party wanting to move, you have the burden of showing the move is necessary and in the best interests of the children. An involuntary job transfer (for you or your present spouse) is a valid reason and most often will result in the move being allowed. The same is true if the move is necessary to deal with a medical condition of you or one of the children, as in the case of the need for a change in climate, to move away from an area where allergies are a problem issue, or moving closer to essential special treatment or care facilities. Wanting to be closer to your family or your spouse's family is much less compelling. Some people cast that reason for a move as having an opportunity to save money by moving to a place where the cost of living is lower or rent is avoided by living with relatives. These arguments are not very successful unless brought on by the other parent's failure to pay court ordered support or maintenance.

Having a valid and compelling reason to move is not the end of the argument on this issue. **There must be a way to fashion a new parenting plan so that the non-moving parent can have the same or close to the same quality of relationship with the children as they had before the move.** If removal of the children is to be allowed, there must be the creation of this new parenting plan. This does not mean that the new plan has to have the same number of overnights or hours of contact that presently occur, but it does mean that consideration must be given to maintaining a quality parent-child relationship, even over geographic distance with patterns of parenting time that meet the logistics of parents living far apart. If you are proposing to move the children away from the other parent, it is absolutely essential that you propose a reasonable, even generous, parenting schedule for the non-moving parent. You must demonstrate that such a schedule is possible and that you will be supportive of the other parent's relationship with the children. Otherwise, your chances of prevailing are greatly diminished.

What is reasonable or generous is measured in part by what the current parenting schedule is and by what contact the non-moving party has actually exercised with the kids prior to the move. If the children live primarily with dad, and mom's parenting schedule is every other weekend from Friday at 6 pm through Sunday at 6 pm plus a few holidays and two weeks in the summer, it is not at all difficult to come up with an equal time schedule weighted heavily toward summer. If mom has a history of exercising only some of her allotted time, then the move is even more likely to be approved and a schedule easily established by which mom can maintain the same level of interaction with the children while at their new residence as she chose to exercise before the move.

A greater difficulty is to come up with a fair, or close to fair, schedule when both parties have engaged in substantial parenting time with the kids and both are actively engaged in the kids' lives as coaches, participants, homework helpers, school volunteers and scout leaders. In these cases, the children are going to lose meaningful parental involvement with at least one parent no matter what the outcome of the issue. That is sad, but it is true. That is why an order permitting a parent to move with the children in these cases should only occur when compelling circumstances require it. Unfortunately, that does not always happen. There are judges with a propensity to allow moves for just about any reason, and there are judges who are prejudiced against moves for all but the most compelling and involuntary reasons. There are judges who favor moms over dads, all else being equal, and some who favor dads over moms. Judges are people too, with human imperfections, personal histories as parents and spouses, and biases and tendencies that are the product of who they are and what they have experienced. That is just the way it is. That is why it is critical to know the judge's tendencies, if the judge has any, through a review of their prior decisions on cases of this type. Ask your lawyer about the judge's history and reputation in removal cases, and if they aren't familiar with them then ask your lawyer to research the matter. That is part of competent representation.

Good preparation and evidence in a relocation case is very much like that developed and presented in custody cases as discussed in Chapter 4. That means if you are the moving party you need to know where you will be living, the location of the nearest parks and recreational centers and the opportunities for each child to continue with the sports they have enjoyed in the past. You need to know who the new dance or music teacher will be. The new pediatrician and pediatric dentist should be identified by you. You should know what school the children will attend if allowed to move, how far it is from your proposed new residence and who their teacher(s) will be. These kinds of details can determine whether a court finds the move to be in the child's best interest.

If you are **opposing a move** of your children out of state, the focus should be on the **negative aspects of the move for the kids**. The biggest negative will, of course, be their diminished time with you if you have been an active presence in their lives. But in addition, negative aspects can include having to leave friends and extended family behind, diminished educational opportunities, having to settle into a new school and community, the time (and risks) of travel to maintain a relationship with both parents, moving to a less desirable neighborhood and inferior housing arrangements. It is important that you present any other negative impact of the proposed move upon the children so the court can consider each as it determines if it is in the best interests of the kids to make the proposed move.

The party opposing the move should also have a contingency plan for a parenting schedule which covers all possible outcomes. If the kids are ordered to move with the other parent, or if the kids are not ordered to move but the other parent moves anyway, a new parenting schedule is necessary. Your proposal for parenting time under each outcome is very important. It shows your priority is to serve the needs of the children, and demonstrates your inherent fairness in being willing to give as much parenting time as you are seeking if the children move.

As you work on formulating a parenting plan to be implemented in the event the other parent moves with or without the children, you will find that you are addressing, in advance, issues that may be a problem in the future. As you consider and propose solutions to travel arrangements and logistics, scheduling, weather contingencies, cost of travel and how to share it, you will be better equipped to deal with those issues when they present themselves as real, not just hypothetical, problems. Formulating a proposed parenting schedule for your kids regardless of which parent is the primary parent requires that you remain kid-focused. That leads to the next issue, one for which there is no happy solution.

When one parent moves to a remote location and both parents were are active in the kids' lives, many parenting schedules, whether entered by agreement or court order, split the summer break equally. This may seem fair on the surface. However, such a plan may prevent your child from any meaningful participation in a summer sport or ongoing activity. This possibility should be considered before parenting orders enter. If you have a child between 10 and 18 years of age who likes to play baseball but will only be in one state or the other for 5 weeks during the summer season because of a split parenting schedule, it will be hard for them to participate on a team in either state where the parents live. Even if allowed, they will only be active for a part of the season. The same is true with all summer team sports and activities. For some kids this is not an issue at all. For others, a split summer may be devastating. Do the best you can to preserve your kids' lives. It will require sacrifice on the part of at least one and perhaps both parents.

When a parent moves a long distance away, other issues arise. Here are some of the most often overlooked questions:

Who pays for transportation?

Who books the plane or bus or train tickets?

If a parent opts to drive themselves and the child to carry out parenting time, do they get reimbursed any of the costs from the other parent?

Do motel stays and meals count as costs of transportation?

Each of these questions needs to be resolved along with the relocation question and the creation of a new parenting schedule.

In assigning costs of transportation, some jurisdictions ignore everything but the relative incomes of the parents and assign those costs in proportion to incomes. Other jurisdictions may consider who caused the new expenses to be created and why, and apportion costs differently. Some jurisdictions ignore the income of a new spouse when determining such matters, and others include it. Raise these issues with your lawyer and be sure you have an understanding of the approach taken in your jurisdiction and by your judge as to each of the issues. One thing is certain: you will want clear and specific terms resolving all of these issues included in any agreement or court order. Quite often an order will not make clear what costs are included, so in an agreement or in a proposed court order, ask for a specific itemization of what costs are to be divided. Orders that are vague, ambiguous, incomplete, or otherwise leave issues to an "agreement of the parties" are bad orders. They create disputes and litigation. Insist that your attorney have all these issues addressed with all the corners filled in. You will be glad you did.

Once the issue of a move is resolved, together with the related issues discussed in the preceding paragraph, it is important to determine if other orders require modification. Orders concerning child support, decision making, and health insurance provisions will all need to be reviewed. If the number of overnights a child spends with either parent changes substantially as a result of the move, then child support should be reviewed and modified in accordance with the law of your jurisdiction. That jurisdiction is the state where the divorce decree was entered, not the new state where the moving party resides. Transportation costs to carry our parenting time may also impact child support. If these will be significant, they will likely impact the level of child support depending upon how they are apportioned between the parties.

In many cases parents share joint decision making for the kids, and they can still do this even if they are not living in close proximity. However, practicality dictates that if there are orders in place requiring the parties to meet, mediate, and otherwise go through steps to resolve an impasse, the difficulties of following those orders when the parties are living in two remote locations may require a change in those orders. In addition, if an order was not already in place allowing either parent to consent to health care for the kids, you will certainly want to have one entered.

Provision of health insurance is often overlooked in relocation cases, though it is an issue of critical importance. Consider the case in which dad, who lives in Colorado, and is not moving, has an HMO covering the kids. The policy is provided by his employer at a reasonable cost. The providers are located in Colorado, New Mexico, Utah, Arizona and California. Mom and the kids move to Hawaii, where dad's HMO has no providers and does not operate. In such cases the parties should consider an order which requires mom to obtain health insurance for the kids in Hawaii, either in addition to or in place of the current coverage. Child support should be adjusted as a result to include a fair sharing of the insurance cost for the kids. Avoid creating a circumstance where large uninsured health care costs for a child emerge because no one thought about this in advance of the move. Remember in your planning that you will need to have coverage in place for the kids that can be used when they are with either parent in either place of residence. That may mean two distinct insurance policies and carriers.

You opposed the move and lost. Now your kids are in California and you are in Kansas. Your child support went up because the kids are with mom more and with you less than before the move. New health insurance costs more than the plan your employer provided and you have to contribute more money for that insurance. What are you supposed to do? I suggest you do what you can to maintain a relationship with your kids. Call them. Send them emails. Never let a birthday or holiday pass without a greeting card from you. Most of all, and I mean this, *write to them*. You remember letter writing. You get a piece of paper and a pen, you sit at a desk or table, and in your own handwriting you create on the paper a story of what is going on in your life that you want to share with your child. You can include pictures, actual printed pictures. Your can email pictures too, but it's not the same. If you have more than one child living away from where you live, even in the same house, write to each child separately. And even better, they will write you back. Send each child half a dozen envelopes with stamps on them, pre-addressed to you. They can use these to send you stuff- a letter, a school paper, a picture, an article in the local paper about their latest achievement, a school schedule, lots of useful stuff. They can do this without asking the other parent for paper or an envelope or a stamp. When you have received back all but one or two envelopes, send another batch. Too many parents with kids living out of state spend more time complaining about how unfair the court order is and what's wrong with their ex and not enough time investing themselves in their kids' lives. Make things better, not worse

If you are the parent who moved away with the kids, be sure to encourage and facilitate all kinds of contact between the kids and the absent parent. Let them know if mom or dad left a message. Absent some really compelling reason, don't open their mail or emails or other communications, but do encourage the kids to share everything with you in a positive way. Facilitating communication is part of the gift of letting your kids know it's ok to love both parents, share things with both parents and have both parents in their lives. If you don't extend a little extra effort to facilitate the long range relationship, you will learn only too soon that no orders concerning children are final, and that a court can rethink its decision based upon whether or not expectations of contact with the absent parent are fulfilled. It is not enough for you to allow the relationship with the other parent. It is your job to **encourage and facilitate** it.

A final and very important issue related to children moving out of state is that of jurisdiction. If the kids move out of state, which court is going to have jurisdiction over future matters to be resolved? There may be more motions dealing with changes in parenting time, another relocation of the children, child support modification, or other child related matters that emerge and need to be resolved. Initially, the court that entered the divorce decree will retain jurisdiction, but there is no guarantee that this will always be the case. There are factors that can lead to a state "ceding " jurisdiction to the state of relocation with the passing of time, including the development of more significant ties to the new community than the old by the children and their primary parent. If you are the parent who did not move you will want any court order to include, in the clearest and strongest language possible, a statement affirming that the court where you live will retain jurisdiction to hear and decide any future issues concerning the children. Discuss this with your attorney, and make sure it is a part of your agenda.

Children who have the presence and positive involvement of both parents in their lives are blessed. That is why I firmly believe that moving children away from a parent that they love should be rare, and only occur when there is literally no alternative available.

Chapter 11
Debts and Bankruptcy

Divorcing your spouse does not mean that you get to divorce your creditors. If you were responsible for paying a debt prior to the divorce, you will be responsible for paying that debt after the divorce even if the divorce orders say your ex-spouse is to pay that debt. Let me repeat that, because it is very important. *If you were responsible for paying a debt prior to the divorce, you will be responsible for paying that debt after the divorce even if the divorce orders say your ex-spouse is to pay that debt.* Creditors are not parties to the divorce action and are not bound by the orders in your divorce case. That can raise some serious problems. Suppose John and Jane have a joint credit card on which they owe $5000.00 at the time of the divorce. The court order says John is to pay the debt, but he doesn't. He gets behind. The credit card company calls Jane and says "we need a payment." Jane will be tempted to say that she doesn't have to pay because the divorce court ordered John to pay the bill. Jane is wrong. Jane can be made to pay. However, if she has properly worded orders, she should be able to recover from John anything she is made to pay on the bill.

Because a divorce court cannot enter orders that exonerate a party from payment of a debt, it is important to have language in your orders that allows you to collect from your ex-spouse any money you pay out for his or her debts and, in addition, be reimbursed for any costs (including legal fees) you incur in dealing with that debt. The language to use in John and Jane's divorce is that John must *indemnify Jane and hold her harmless on any and all debts John is required to pay by the terms of the order (or agreement).*

What this means is that if Jane has to pay off a debt John was to pay, she can bring an action against John in the divorce action (or a separate action) to recover the money she paid out. In addition, if she incurred legal fees or court costs in dealing with the debt and in seeking reimbursement from John, she can collect those as well. If Jane borrowed money in her own name to cover John's debt and incurs interest, then she can recover the interest paid as well. Even if Jane had the cash to cover John's debt, she can also recover reasonable interest on the funds she paid out until she is repaid. By having the indemnification language in the orders, a party is protected to a degree, but that protection might be lost if the party ordered to pay the debt files bankruptcy.

If a party to a divorce is ordered to pay certain debts, that party can still file a bankruptcy and be relieved of the obligation to pay those debts. However, child support and maintenance payments, whether past or future, **cannot** be discharged in the bankruptcy. One way to argue against discharge of a debt in bankruptcy is to argue that the debt is *in the nature of* child support or spousal maintenance or family support. This book is not intended to get into the finer points of such legal issues, but you do want to be aware of this option. One area where that argument has been effective is that of medical bills for children. If the parties incur medical bills for a child not covered by insurance (either before or after the divorce is final) and the orders assign any portion of them to the party filing bankruptcy, the other party may be successful in arguing that the bankrupt party's contribution on those debts is *in the nature of* child support. Consult your attorney on this point, and perhaps engage a bankruptcy specialist to assist with the issue, especially if the amount of money involved is significant.

Some further protection against getting stuck without a remedy in the event your ex-spouse files for bankruptcy can be accomplished by including additional language in your divorce agreement or court order. That language should recite that the entire settlement (or court order) assumes that neither party will be filing a bankruptcy. It should then state that if either party does file a bankruptcy, all terms of the agreement are subject to review and modification in light of any debt discharge in the bankruptcy. Different lawyers use different language on this issue, and you should confer with your lawyer as to their preference. However, you will want some term to cover this contingency. In some instances the fact that a party is relieved of paying substantial debt will mean that that party can afford to pay more maintenance. The non-bankrupting party can certainly demonstrate a need for more maintenance because they now have more debt to pay than was anticipated at the time the divorce orders entered. Proper language may let the non-bankrupting party recover additional maintenance in order to help them to pay those debts they were not expected to pay before the bankruptcy filing. If your lawyer is not familiar with language to use, suggest she or he confer with someone who does. Alternatively, you can engage a bankruptcy lawyer to assist in drafting the agreement or proposed order.

In addition to the indemnification clause and the language dealing with the possibility of bankruptcy, other provisions in the orders should include a deadline to refinance or pay off each debt that one party is ordered to pay so that the other party is no longer liable on the debt. In the case of a loan secured by a house or a car, if the pay-off or refinancing of the loan does not occur by the required date, I like to include a provision that the asset securing the loan is to be sold and the proceeds of sale are to pay off the debt secured by the property. Always add that if the sale proceeds are insufficient to pay off the balance owed, the balance shall be paid solely by the party who was ordered to pay the debt in the original orders. You want the clearest possible statement of who is to pay which debts. Do not rely on any implications. Spell it out. List every debt by account name and number and approximate balance owed. Assign every debt to one party or the other. If each party is to pay a certain portion of a particular debt, state the dollar amount for each.

You might become liable for debts assigned to the other party that are not paid by that party in the event that other party dies before the debt is paid. It happens. When you formulate a settlement agreement or a proposed order that you are asking the court to enter, you will always want a life insurance policy on the life of the other party with you named as the beneficiary. The face amount of the policy should be sufficient to provide for a benefit equal to future maintenance and child support that would have been paid under the orders if the obligor had not died. The obligor should pay the premiums, but you will want the insurance company to notify you in the event of non-payment so you can pay the premium to keep the policy in effect. Nearly all lawyers are aware of and attend to that matter. However, in my experience quite a few lawyers fail to include in that life insurance policy amount the unpaid debts assigned to the obligor. That is the amount of debt assigned to the other party that you responsible for if they do not pay it. When you determine how much life insurance you want the other party to maintain, add that debt amount to the amount that is needed to cover child support and spousal maintenance. Remind your lawyer to do this.

Let's assume a simple case in which the husband is to pay the wife maintenance for ten years at $1000.00 per month, pay her child support for one child that is anticipated to be paid for 15 years at $600.00 per month., and he is also is also ordered to pay $40,000.00 in marital debt on which the wife is potentially liable to the creditors if for any reason the husband does not pay. The total amount that the husband will pay if they fulfill all orders is $120,000.00 in maintenance plus $108,000.00 in child support plus $40,000.00 in debts, a total of $268,000.00 over time. You should ask for a life insurance policy in that amount as the initial amount of life insurance to be maintained for your benefit. The figure could be a little lower due to present value discount and tax implications- but keep it simple. Add the numbers and ask for that amount.

Even taking every precautionary measure discussed in this chapter, circumstances may leave you stuck with debt that the other party was supposed to pay. The reason may be a bankruptcy, a death, or just having a deadbeat for an ex-spouse. If the obligations are overwhelming, you too may want to consider a bankruptcy. Bankruptcy is a highly specialized area of the law. If you have to file for bankruptcy because you find yourself facing an overwhelming financial situation, I recommend you retain a lawyer who specializes in bankruptcy to guide you in that process.

Chapter 12
The Job Isn't Over 'Til the Paperwork's Done

You have heard the phrase " The job isn't over 'til the paperwork's done" in a variety of contexts. I remember it in a cartoon. A picture of an unoccupied toilet seat with a roll of paper hanging next to it bore that caption. That statement is true in the bathroom, in business, and in divorce. Divorce orders create the rules that govern the parties and spell out what each is supposed to do. The doing of what is ordered usually requires some formal paperwork. I have been retained by people whose divorce was finalized years earlier because they needed help obtaining a car title, prepare a deed transferring property ownership, or obtaining their share of a pension plan. Doing these things years after the orders were entered can be time consuming and costly. It is much more efficient to do them at the time the divorce is final. All properly drawn settlement agreements and court orders will contain a provision which requires each party to sign all documents necessary to carry out the terms of the court's orders. Be sure your orders or agreements contain that requirement, and include a provision that if you need to take legal action to make the other party do what they should have done, that you are entitled to have them reimburse you for all legal fees and costs you incur in the process.

Creating, signing, and, where necessary, recording the documents to transfer property ought to be done as quickly as possible following the divorce and before you discharge your attorney or before your attorney is allowed to withdraw. Transferring property that requires a written document of title is not difficult. For real estate you will need a form of written deed which your attorney can prepare. Have your lawyer do this on all real estate that you are to receive. Do not rely on opposing counsel to prepare a deed to property you are to receive. When you are presented a deed to real estate that is to be the property of the other party, read it for accuracy and then sign and return it. There is no reason to play around with it or delay the signing. Most jurisdictions have a provision in the law that if you don't sign a real estate deed you are ordered to sign the other side can get an order that directs the clerk of the court to sign it for you, and the deed is valid. That process takes time and is costly, and the court will assess the costs and fees against you. That is, you will be paying the opposing lawyer hundreds if not thousands of dollars to do what you could have and should have done at no cost to anyone. Just sign the deed or deeds. If your ex-spouse refuses to sign a real estate deed, ask your attorney to carry out this process, making sure to request reimbursement of all legal fees and costs from the other party.

Once the deed transferring real estate to you from the other party has been signed, do not forget to record the deed with the county official in charge of recording deeds, in the county *where the property is located*. You must record where the property is located, even if you reside in a different county.

Transfer of automobiles or other titled vehicles such as trailers, motorcycles, and RVs is done by signing the title over to the other party. If the vehicle has a loan against it, you likely do not have possession of the title that you can sign, so you will sign a document called something like "Power of Attorney as to Motor Vehicle" or perhaps a "Bill of Sale." Each state has a preferred manner of doing such transfers, but they are always done with a written document. As with real estate, be sure your own lawyer prepares the documents for items that are to be your property. When presented with documents to transfer property to your ex-spouse, read them for accuracy and then sign and return without delay.

If a party refuses to cooperate with signing a vehicle title or other transfer document, the appropriate remedy is to seek a contempt of court citation. This process involves telling the court that an order was entered, the other party had the ability to do what the order required, and they refused to do it. The court then issues a citation, something like a ticket or summons, to the non-complying party and there will be a hearing. If found in contempt, the offending party will be made to pay all legal fees and costs incurred by the other party, and will be ordered to do what the orders require. In addition, they may be fined or even jailed for their willful disobedience of the court's order. The contempt process is appropriate to enforce any orders of the court.

Pension and profit sharing plans, as well as 401k plans and IRAs, are divided or transferred by a document called a Qualified Domestic Relations Order, or QDRO for short. The QDRO takes a plan and divides it as directed in the divorce orders or agreement. A separate QDRO is required for each plan to be divided, whether an IRA, a pension plan, a 401k plan, or other similar plans. Some lawyers regularly prepare these documents as part of their practice, and others never do. They prefer to hire a person who specializes in preparing the QDRO. In practice, hiring a third party expert to prepare the QDRO may be cheaper than paying your attorney his hourly rate. Most preparers will charge between $500.00 and $700.00 (2010 dollars) for each QDRO they prepare. Each plan, whether a private pension or public employment retirement plan, has its own unique rules. IRAs and 401k plans are easier, but still require compliance with fairly strict rules for content and form. Whether your attorney prepares the QDRO s or a third party expert prepares them, you want them to start the process as soon as possible following the entry of the final divorce. This process takes a while to complete.

If you are to receive a portion of a retirement plan, 401k plan or IRA that is in the other party's name, you will want to notify the plan administrator immediately that there is a court order dividing the plan and that a QDRO will follow. The plan administrator should be sent a copy of the divorce decree and orders. Most will acknowledge receipt and "freeze" the plan until a QDRO is received, approved, and implemented. If you are the participant in the plan to be divided, you will want the QDRO done as soon as possible so your plan or IRA gets "unfrozen." Preparation, obtaining approval for, and having a QDRO issued by the court requires the cooperation of both parties. Failure to cooperate can subject the offending party to contempt proceedings and penalties.

Once a QDRO has been drafted, it is sent to the plan administrator for approval. That plan administrator will either approve the document or list changes necessary for approval. Once a final form is approved, it is submitted to the court and enters as a court order. Once the order is entered, there is still more to be done. A certified copy of the QDRO needs to be sent to the plan administrator. The party who is receiving a piece of the other party's plan (or their attorney) needs to follow up to confirm that the order has been carried out and funds transferred or a new account created for the recipient.

Other paperwork to be completed once the divorce is final includes being sure the court enters the written final orders and Decree of Divorce. Most courts rely on counsel to prepare and submit in written form the orders the court pronounces. Some lawyers do this efficiently and accurately. Others do not. Ask your lawyer about the status of final written and signed orders and decree if you ever have a question.

Some divorce orders require the parties to file a joint tax return for at least one tax year. The orders should also specify how any taxes owed are to be divided between the parties and how any refund is to be shared by the parties. Select a reputable and neutral party to do such tax returns. Get your documentation to the preparer early, and get the returns done. If the other party is not cooperative, talk to your attorney about filing a contempt action.

Many divorce orders require a party to show proof of health insurance for the children and provide insurance cards and claim submission information to the other party. The orders may require a party to maintain insurance on their life naming the other party as beneficiary and show proof that the policy is in effect. Properly worded orders will state a deadline for provision of these kinds of information. Insist on timely or early compliance. If you are the party who has to obtain the health insurance or life insurance, once you have done so your obligation is not fulfilled until you provide the information, in writing, to the other party. The job isn't over 'til the paperwork's done.

Within days of your divorce being final, you should sit down with a paper and pen (or laptop) and read through the orders. List every obligation you have to fulfill and when it has to be accomplished. Make a separate list of everything your ex-spouse has to do, and the dates they are to be accomplished. Check off each item as it is done. If some things require multiple steps, make notes of each step. For example, if you need a real estate deed transferring title to you, you might want to list it as three events: 1) send deed to ex-spouse to sign; 2) receive signed deed from ex-spouse; and 3) record deed. Remember, the job isn't over 'til the paperwork's done.

Final Thoughts

Self inflicted wounds leave the worst scars of all. Avoid those types of scars by dealing with the issues in your divorce in a businesslike and dispassionate manner with the assistance of competent counsel.

- Protect yourself from all conceivable contingencies by concise and comprehensive agreements or orders.

- Don't play games with money and assets.

- Don't use the kids as a means to justify yourself.

- Don't argue just for the sake of arguing.

- Don't oppose something just because the other party proposed it.

- Don't overburden everyone you know with every negative thought you have about your ex or future ex.

- Play fair. Disclose all relevant information.

- Follow court orders. If you don't like them, ask the court to change them.

- Keep divorce simple by keeping your new friends and lovers out of it.

- If you or your ex-spouse has to move away, focus on what is best for the kids and problem solve rather than re-litigating everything, even if it means you just have to make the best of a bad situation that is not your fault.

- Follow through to see that all orders are carried out and all paperwork is completed.

Divorce happens. No two people are the same and no two divorce actions are the same. As one local law firm in my town says in their television ads, every case they handle has "special circumstances." That is exactly right. As a result, not every suggestion in this book may be appropriate to every issue in every case, and may not be appropriate to every issue in your case. As you were reading a particular chapter or a paragraph on a particular issue, you may have thought, "That's fine, but there is no way I can do that." More likely you were thinking, " That's fine, but there is no way my A- - H- - - spouse will ever do that." You might be right. But don't start with that negative perspective. Try to take the high road for your sake, not your spouse's. Control what you can control and don't worry about trying to control the other party. Focus on the issues. Focus on your communication with family and others. Focus on your disclosure of information, your diligence in fulfilling orders. Things will be better, or at least less bad, if you do.

There is an old joke that asks "Why do divorces cost so much?" The answer given is "Because they are worth it." Benjamin Franklin once said that paying taxes to the government made him feel patriotic, but that he was pretty sure that he'd feel just as patriotic even if he paid less in taxes. I think you will value your divorce just as much even if it costs you less in money, in time, and in emotion. I hope that this book helps reduce the cost to you in all three of these areas.

Acknowledgements

My deepest thanks to my wife, Debra Jacobson for content suggestions, masterful proofreading and corrections, and for staying married to me for almost 30 years as of publication date. Thanks to Deborah Ingram, family friend and English teacher for additional editing and also for content suggestions. My sister-in- law Mary Tully, former English professor and teacher, offered valuable content suggestions. Her husband, Mike Tully, retired lawyer, also made many suggestions, a few of which were actually helpful. Finally, to the hundreds of clients who taught me as much about divorce as I ever taught them, thank you for the privilege of working with you and for you. None of the comments in this book are about you unless they are positive comments. All the negative examples are from those people you divorced.